Little Creek Press
5341 Sunny Ridge Road
Mineral Point, WI 53565

ORDERING INFORMATION
**Quantity sales.** Special discounts are available on quantity purchases by corporations, associations, and others. For details, contact info@littlecreekpress.com

**Orders by US trade bookstores and wholesalers.**
Please contact Little Creek Press or Ingram for details.

Printed in the United States of America

Cataloging-in-Publication Data
Names: Waldinger, Joy Elisabeth, author. Serene, Akira, illustrator
Title: Trash Crab
Description: Mineral Point, WI: Little Creek Press, 2023.
Identifiers: LCCN: 2022918513 | ISBN: 978-1-955656-37-5
Subjects: JUVENILE NONFICTION / Animals / Animal Welfare

Book design by Akira Serene and Little Creek Press

# TRASH CRAB

Written by J. Eliza Wall (Joy Elisabeth Waldinger)

Illustrated by Akira Serene

LITTLE CREEK PRESS®
AND BOOK DESIGN
MINERAL POINT, WISCONSIN

## Akira Serene
Illustrator

**Akira Serene** is an artist and educator who believes art can help, heal, educate, and communicate. She learned how to paint when she was merely ten years old, rushing home after school to watch Bob Ross, and realized in high school that she wanted to be a teacher. She received her BFA in painting from the Pennsylvania Academy of the Fine Arts and her Master of Arts in Teaching in Visual Arts from the University of the Arts. Her illustrations focus on portraiture, character design, introspective mental health topics, and storytelling. She teaches her students and two daughters (Zoë and Margot) the importance of using one's voice to make a positive change in the world. This book reminds us that we can all make a difference, no matter how small, and it is dedicated to her daughters and students, who are the future of the planet.

## J. Eliza Wall
Writer

**J. Eliza Wall** (Joy Elisabeth Waldinger) is a Philadelphia artist, writer, filmmaker, and art educator. Her work explores family dynamics, the human condition, nostalgia, and reconnection to nature. She has many pets in her tiny South Philly home: Ryder the pug beagle mix, Leon the chameleon, Orville the goldfish, Speck the jade snail, and Kat and June the hermit crabs. Her short films have won awards in national and international film festivals. She has been published in a variety of literary magazines and is a volunteer curator for Button Poetry. Her first children's book was *Like the Sun Holds the Moon: A Children's Book*, and her first novel is *Like The Sun Holds The Moon: A Novel*. She believes art is a powerful tool that can generate change and healing locally and globally.

Dedicated to
future block captains,
inventors, artists, scientists,
and creative little kids
everywhere who want to
change the world!

The Taylor sisters started their summer day like any other,

Katerina Mae "Kat"

Juniper Rose "June"

with sunshine, snacks, and seashells.

Until one day, when their seaside hangout

turned into a search and rescue mission

Humans throw away trillions of tons of garbage every year, and ocean creatures are among the worst affected by it. You can get rid of waste and protect your environment by **reducing, reusing, and recycling.**

June quickly found that the coastline was crawling
with trash crabs and other creatures

that needed to be saved
from garbage that was
washing up on the shore.

A **Trash Crab** uses plastic bottle caps, cans, and other garbage to protect itself, but it can get stuck inside these items. Don't collect shells. Leave them for the crabs, and take the trash instead.

It made her happy to save
the animals from the trash,

and they appreciated
her support.

But as she was collecting, she
found more and more animals in
need of a helping hand!

Many sea creatures get caught in plastic that makes its way into our oceans. You can help by cutting plastic rings before throwing them away!

Realizing that she could not do it alone,

she hollered for
her sister Kat

who knew just what to do.

A **community cleanup**, even if it's just two people, brings volunteers together to clean, repair, and improve public spaces like beaches. Working together makes a difference in the world!

They soon discovered that they had
their work cut out for them.

Birds can quickly become tangled in fishing line, and it can wrap around their legs, bills, or wings and stop them from flying and looking for food. Go birding or snorkeling instead of catch-and-release fishing.

They continued to follow the trail of trash down the coast.

Seabirds, turtles, and whales often eat litter along our coastlines. Researchers estimate that about 524,000 pounds of plastic wash up on beaches. So be sure to clean up after yourself if you are hanging out on the beach, and tell your friends and family to do the same!

It stretched on for miles.

But they were determined
to do everything they could

to make things better.

Their mission took them
into the water,

Sea turtles can't tell the
difference between plastic
bags and jellyfish and
accidentally eat them,
which makes them sick!
Use reusable bags to cut
down on plastic waste!

where the problem only seemed to
get bigger and harder to fix.

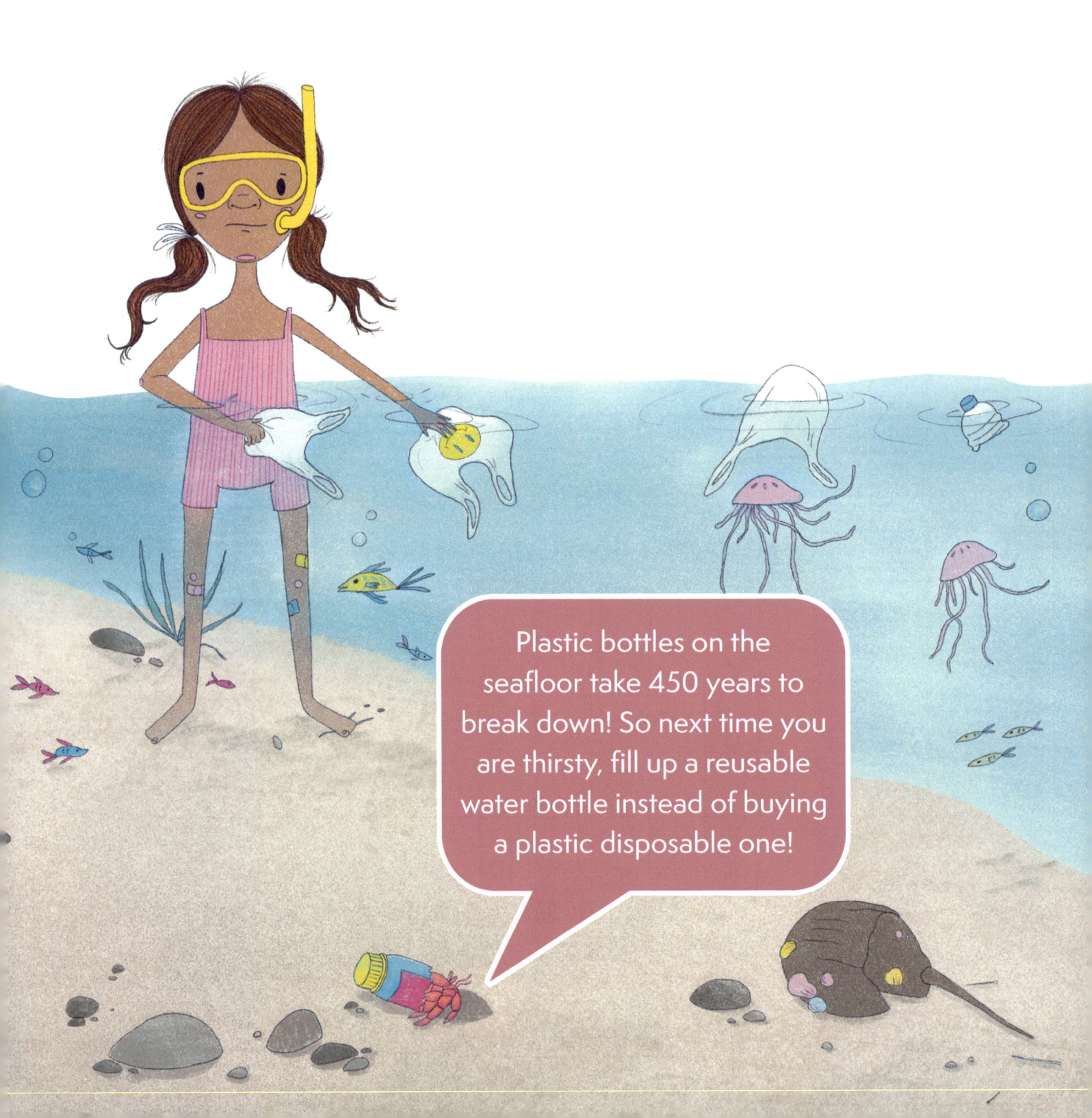

Plastic bottles on the seafloor take 450 years to break down! So next time you are thirsty, fill up a reusable water bottle instead of buying a plastic disposable one!

They quickly lost track of time,

as their journey seemed to get more and more complicated.

When fishing gear gets lost, it becomes "ghost gear." Almost half of the **Great Pacific Garbage Patch** is made up of fishing nets. Ghost gear can continue to catch ocean animals long after being abandoned. This is known as a "ghost catch."

They headed home as the sun was setting.

Before they went inside, they sorted through everything they had collected on their walk.

Instead of tossing everything out, they decided to make some magic from the scraps of plastic that had washed up on shore.

Our world's trash problem needs **creative problem-solvers** who can find new ideas. Use your imagination to come up with unique solutions to save our planet!

The next day, they hit the beach early with their new inventions, ready to make some change!

**Upcycling**, also known as creative reuse, is a fun way to turn unwanted materials, recycling, or trash into new inventions that reduce waste in our oceans and landfills. It's time to make trash into treasure!

Now it's your turn!

## REDUCE REUSE RECYCLE

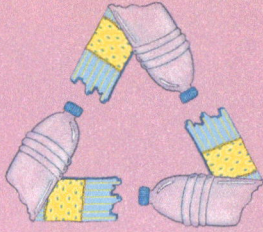

The three Rs are helpful to reduce the amount of pollution and waste in our world by limiting our use of various items, reusing things, and recycling objects.

## TRASH CRAB

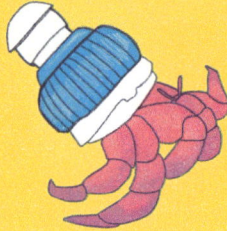

A trash crab is a hermit crab that uses plastic bottle caps, cans, and other garbage to protect itself since its environment has changed. They can get stuck inside these items and get hurt.

## COMMUNITY CLEANUP

A community cleanup brings people together to clean, repair, and improve public spaces like beaches. If you live in the city, you can be a junior block captain who helps make their neighborhoods clean.

## GREAT PACIFIC GARBAGE PATCH

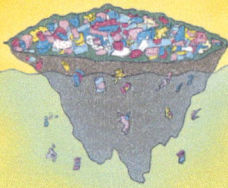

The Great Pacific Garbage Patch is the largest collection of ocean plastic in the world. Trash trapped there is harmful to animals, as it grows bigger each day. It's located between Hawaii and California.

## CREATIVE PROBLEM-SOLVING

Creative problem-solving is a way of solving problems or identifying opportunities when a problem comes up. It encourages you to find new ideas using your imagination to reach your goals.

## UPCYCLE

Upcycling is when you take something normally recycled and transform it into something more valuable. Upcycling is a fun way to reduce the amount of garbage we make.

# How can We Make Our World a better place?

## SUSTAINABLE DEVELOPMENT GOALS

| | | | | | |
|---|---|---|---|---|---|
| No Poverty | Zero Hunger | GOOD Health and Well-being | Quality Education | Gender Equality | Clean Water and Sanitation |
| Affordable and Clean Energy | Decent Work and Economic Growth | Industry Innovation and Infrastructure | Reduced Inequalities | Sustainable Cities and Communities | Responsible Consumption and Production |
| Climate Action | Life Below Water | Life On Land | Peace, Justice and Strong Institutions | Partnerships for the goals | Sustainable Development GOALS |

These goals are the blueprint for protecting the planet and improving the lives of everyone, everywhere. In 2015, all United Nations Member States adopted these goals, setting a 15-year plan to achieve them. They address the global challenges we face, including climate action, education, poverty, peace, justice, and many more!